M

for

Mums

By

Lyn Franklin

Published by
Home Life Publishing
e-mail:
homelifepublishing@hotmail.co.uk

ISBN 978-0-9552484-0-5

0-9552484-0-X

CONTENTS

FOREWORD

I think of myself as a modern middle-aged mum, being the age when I am also embracing the values of the two generations either side of my own.

Throughout my long marriage, our daughter and son have been an enduring source of interest, pleasure, challenge and support as they have grown into adults.

Aimed mainly at mums, my writing reflects the trials and tribulations of family life and although I do tackle serious topics, I often try to inject a bit of humour into my work, as I think laughter is far too often lacking in our lives nowadays.

I am not pretentious enough to describe this as a book of poetry, rather a collection of thoughts or observations. I like to write in an accessible way about everyday things to which people can easily relate.

I hope, therefore, that you gain some simple enjoyment from dipping into this book.

With thanks to
my friends
Simon, Barbara and Chris
for their encouragement

and to my family
for inspiring much
of my writing

MOTHERING SUNDAY

There's no need to buy me presents
All on one day
With awkward greetings
And nothing to say
Spread them out across the year
And help to give me all round cheer
Just the odd cup of tea
Or a kiss on the cheek
A straightened cushion
Or a meal once a week
The opened garage
When I am in pain
Or a hand with the shopping
In the pouring rain
The windows cleaned inside
Or a curtain pulled nicely
A worktop wiped over
Or a towel hung precisely
I don't mean to sound hard
Or somewhat ungrateful
And I hope you won't think
That this poem is hateful
I *do* appreciate the presents you buy me
And *do* understand the loving behind them
But it's the little things often
Which mean so much
And sometimes they alone
Are just enough

*I just wanted to say that there was no need
to buy me expensive gifts*

BEDTIMES

If I could find the answer to bedtimes
I'd be rich
I'd no longer have to stand there
With me nerves all of a twitch
Persuading and cajoling
To get them near the sink
I'd have lots of time
To just sit down and think .....
About a sundrenched island
Where I could be alone
Away from nightly arguments
Where I can't hear them moan
That they're too tired to get undressed
Or clean their bloomin' teeth
I'd drift into another world
Of perfect colour hues
Where all the children stood in line
Awaiting for the loos
And quickly washed their faces
And jumped straight into bed
But then, I suppose ....
I'd be dead!

*When my children were young, it used
to take ages to get them into bed, so
one evening I wrote this poem*

MISSING YOU

It's strange when you're away
The house is kind of bare
I keep turning corners
Expecting to find you there
I miss your late night vigil
Upon the toilet seat
And the distant pitter patter
Of your heffalumping feet
Your laughing and your crying
When you have had a fight
Or when you've had a nightmare
Your calling out at night
I miss you in a thousand ways
That only we could share
In laughter and in anger
In joy and in despair
Your kind and thoughtful nature
Your aggravating moods
Your loving and consoling
Or even when you're rude
I miss you in the mornings
When you are slow to wake
I miss your bedtime tantrums
When it is getting late
But most of all I miss you
Because you're who you are
My daughter and my friend
The best I have, by far

*I wrote this when my daughter went on
a school trip abroad at the age of eleven*

MESS

I know it's the mess that depresses me
The problem is mess to excess
I know it's the mess that distresses me
When it's often the mess of the rest
I flounder in procrastination
My feelings I cannot express
But I know it's the mess that depresses me
When I can't make the mess any less!

*For everyone who, like me, is at a loss to
know where to put everything that you
accumulate in a family house!*

WALKING

Step out, leave behind the frenzy of the walls.
They say you should study the wondrous
shape of nature when you are feeling low.
But other things can lift your spirits too.
The poignant cooing of the wood pigeons
hidden in the trees just drains away your
stress and relaxes your body; the gentle
rustling of leaves in the breeze, and the
earthy smell of warm grass; the momentary
scent of a fox or the evocative perfume of
jasmine clinging to the wall, and to your
mind, returning you to the Mediterranean
and happier times.

As you walk, you drift in and out of
consciousness, like a waking sleep, and
allow the lateral thinking to take over.
Your thoughts hover briefly before flitting
onwards and upwards into the sky, like a
silver bird. This is the time when decisions
are made and problems solved. Brilliant
ideas come to you as you free yourself of
the shackles of realism. The exploration is
wonderful and you feel exultant at the
possibilities.

So remember, these are your personal
treasures you can return to, which
rejuvenate your body and soul, each time
you go walking.

*I wrote this one day because I wanted to
express how therapeutic walking can be in
clearing your mind*

ODE TO A PLUMBER

Me thinks a plumber
Is a very special breed
For they are most elusive
When their services you need
Where *do* they all go
Is it to a Plumbers' Club
Or are they merely fixing leaks
Down at the local pub?
Persistence seems the answer
When you have sprung a leak
Even if you have to phone
Seven days a week
For when you've waited in
At the appointed time
And by the close of day
Again there's been no sign
You must just keep on trying
You'll get there in the end
Even if it drives you
Very nearly round the bend

Sheer frustration prompted this
particular poem and I left a copy
for my plumber to read too
(when he eventually arrived)!

SNOOKERED

Our postman looks just like Steve Davis
Though he goes by the name of Keith
I guess a job away from the glare
Gives him a sense of relief
From all the hectic lifestyle
That comes with snooker fame
Of public recognition
And calling out of his name
I expect he became a postman
To gain anonymity
Being out and about really early
Must help to make him feel free
I'm so pleased he delivers to *our* house
When sometimes I'm making my tea
But there's no need to worry I'll tell on you Steve
Your secret is safe with me!

I wrote this to amuse our postman

INFLUENTIAL FRIENDS

I worry about the future
The present goes so fast
I feel bewildered by my life
Trying to hold on to the past
Like a car going out of control
My direction I have lost
My daughter seems no longer mine
And I must pay the cost
I'm frightened that I cannot cope
The guidelines all have changed
It seems like all my principles
Are suddenly re-arranged
I'm trying desperately to find
A way out of this maze
To overcome the problems
Of this very awkward phase
But I only seem to flounder
At every twist and turn
I suppose that I must trust
That I will come to learn

*When your children go to
secondary education, all the
'goalposts' suddenly seem to
be moved, and this can be
somewhat disconcerting!*

ADOLESCENCE

Who is this stranger
Who lies within our midst?
Do I know where he's come from
Or where he is going?
What are the things that make him exist?
If only I could see within his mind
What would I find?
What lingers there
Unknown to me?
I know not where to start
To reach into his heart
I cannot help him free
If he won't talk to me
I want to help uncover
The things that cause him pain
But of course he cannot tell
Because I am his mother

*For any parent with teenagers, I think this
poem speaks for itself*

KEEPING TRACK

I hope you don't think
That I don't care
When you're away
Somewhere out there
I'm trying to be
A really cool mum
Which I can tell you
Is not much fun
I have a feeling
You think it's a doddle
Because you believe
I've nowt in my noddle
What you don't understand
What you can't see
Is I'd be less controlling
If you were straight with me
I'm sure that your friends
Think I'm a real pain
But they don't have the problem
Of finding you *again!*

*I was endeavouring to be a
responsible parent at the time!*

IF ONLY THE CAT COULD TALK

We came home at dead of night
If only the cat could talk
All was peaceful, all was quiet
If only the cat could talk
The kitchen was surprisingly neat
If only the cat could talk
We wondered if they'd **bothered** to eat
If only the cat could talk
The silent amp sat in the lounge
*If **only** the cat could talk*
And from the rooms there was no sound
If only the cat could talk
The bedroom lights were all turned off
If only the cat could talk
Not even a snigger or a cough
If only the cat could talk
But at the early break of day
The bathroom stood in disarray
The tell-tale signs lay on the mat
But this was not a sickly **cat**!
The empty bottles later spied
Were testament to youthful pride
Nothing was said or yet denied
*If **only** the cat could talk!*

This poem was inspired by the serenity of our cat when I let her out into the garden that night

THE LIAR

Is it the truth
Or is it a lie?
Do you know the difference anymore?
Can I trust what you say
Or is it for me to judge?
Just put the onus on to somebody else to decide

When it matters
Can I trust?
Can I believe what you say?
You no longer know do you?
It's just a game you play
You can lie to the world
But the inescapable truth is
You cannot lie to yourself

In my experience, there is nothing
more frustrating than trying to get
to the truth of a situation

THE CRISIS

Would we be laughing years from now?
Would we be quoting anecdotes at some
significant function or reminiscing in
someone's kitchen over a late-night glass of
wine? How will this episode in our lives
unfold?

The only way I can withstand the barrage
now is to see it in that long term context;
trying to see the bigger picture – not easy
when you're in the middle of the frame,
feeling that your whole life has been put
under the microscope and become focused
on just this one thing.

But I have to trust it will move on. Like a
log jammed in the river which one day just
gently drifts away downstream, we will
move on.

*When we experience a crisis in our lives, it
can feel all consuming at the time*

TURNING THE TABLES

Sunday morning
And how the tables are turned
Twice now he's tried to wake his father
Amusing and incongruous it sounds
Like *he* is the parent
And his dad
The recalcitrant son
"I've got to go in ten minutes," he says
In that meaningful tone that we adopt
On school days to him
Will it be effective I wonder
Or will he be late for work?
Again he calls, just to check that
Late-night dad has made it out of bed
I know he will, because the promise
Of a cooked breakfast lures him to town
But first he has to deliver the chef!

This was when our son was dependent
on Dad for a lift to work for his weekend job

RESULTS DAY

I stood as an observer, there but not there,
in the leafy sunlight so special to the
morning, trying to take it all into my
memory, as I knew this would be a day to
recall.

Like a movie camera, my eyes watched the
darting figures running to greet each other,
embracing one another - and with every
blink, I took a snapshot of the scene.

This was a memorable day when all they
had been working towards for so many
years was coming to fruition. Some
shrieked with delight, others stood quietly
waiting. Other parents lingered like me,
hovering in that limbo land of adolescence.
I knew I wanted to be there although I had no
purpose beyond support or congratulation.

Where had the years gone? I closed my
eyes and the snapshots clicked through my
mind; from birth, to toddler, to school and
suddenly this; so quickly, too quickly, to
this.

*Written to mark one of the milestones in
school life, that of receiving GCSE results*

THE GAP YEAR

I know when you go I shall miss you
Though your presence will be in the air
I'll miss your mess in the bathroom
And the dirty clothes everywhere
I'll miss your exuberant nature
And your cold dismissive glare
Your enthusiastic passion
And the wonderful smell of your hair

But I'll think of you whilst you're away dear
And the sights you'll see out there
The joy of your independence
And the people you'll meet everywhere
You know I will worry about you
But I know that you will take care
And I *do* understand why you're going
So please take my love with you there

The gap year can be a heart-wrenching
experience for some parents

WHY ARE WE LIKE WE ARE?

Why are we like we are?
Does any of us know?
Is it all in the genes
Or is it from schemes
That started long ago?

Are we hollow beings
Right at the start
And somebody fills in the blanks?
Are we made from ourselves
Or from somebody else
Pushing away at the flanks?

What forms our minds
In such a way
To make us feel
Weak or strong?
Who can tell
What life has to deal
And if it is right or wrong?

We just have to be
To let ourselves see
What life will slowly unravel
To learn from mistakes
From joy and heartbreaks
But that is the road we must travel

Is it nurture or nature, I wonder?

THE UNI DEBATE

Don't push me into a corner
From which I cannot escape
To trample on my feelings
Would be a big mistake
For it's *my* life we're talking of
My future happiness
Please let me choose the route I want
To take me to success
I know you want the best for me
And all you say is true
But still, you must remember
That I am *me*, not you.

*I wrote this short poem in the early hours of
the morning following one of those long late-
night kitchen conversations which evolve
from nowhere*

THE BEDROOM

I like to think of myself as a well-adjusted
parent but now my grown-up children are
at that stage of coming and going from
home – to return to university or to travel to
far off climes (as they are inclined to do
these days), I always find it difficult to step
into their bedrooms that first time after
they have gone. Invariably, the bed
remains unmade, just as they got out of it,
and their clothes and possessions are lying
around, as though they are about to return
later that day. I don't know what is worse –
for it to be left in this state of disarray or to
be neatly tidied, as if to underline their
going. Either way, it is a very emotional
step to take to walk in there and suddenly
be aware that they are not returning for a
while.

Are other mothers like me? If my children
are travelling long and far, I tend to leave
things as they are for a bit, to allow myself
to adjust to their going. The thought of
sweeping up their dirty clothes straight into
the washing machine is unbearable, as
though to eradicate their memory. I believe
it to be a very basic animal instinct to want
to retain something of your children in their
absence which still bears their special
aroma and, in some small way, keeps the
connection between you. It's that sense of
loss, that fear of losing them, which I
imagine every parent must feel about their
children. Of course, I *do* adjust after a
while to their going, but initially it is very
hard to take that first step into the
bedroom.

Maybe not all mothers are as sentimental as I am

19

A KISS

There are times when I would kiss you
But I know that you'd want more
And I don't want to hurt you
By having to withdraw
It's not like when we started
When a kiss was just enough
To whip us to a frenzy
Of mad and passionate love
A luxurious siesta
Would follow on from there
With no responsibilities
Our lives were free of care
But now there are so many things
To occupy our time
It's often very difficult
To find the frame of mind
To switch to being sexy
In the middle of it all
When I'm trying to cook the dinner
And the kids are in the hall
So yes, I'd like to kiss you
To express to you my love
But sometimes I avoid it
Cos I know it's not enough

To kiss or not to kiss?

THE GREAT PEE DEBATE

Why don't some men ever wash their hands
When visiting the loo?
Is turning the tap on and lifting the soap
So very hard to do?

When I get in a state
And dare to ask my mate
To help me to try to understand
His favourite retort
So very sweet and short
Is that men do not pee upon their hands

But when they're in retreat
They must *have* to lift the seat
If a female has just been there before them
So bacteria must linger
Upon their little fingers
And it's to *all* our peril
They ignore them!

*With apologies to all those men who **do**
wash their hands!*

IN THE SHOWER

Do you talk to yourself in the shower (like
men are said to cry in solace on
motorways)? They say it's the first sign of
madness – talking to yourself, but I
disagree.

There's a certain therapy in articulating
your feelings camouflaged by the sound of
running water and a loud electric pump.
More prudent perhaps to commit your
innermost thoughts to an unhearing,
unanswering device (although there seems
to be one of those in my house already)!

Vent your anger in the steamy atmosphere
of your ablutions, or softly sob in the
caressing warmth of the water, which
washes away your tears, leaving no trace of
a broken heart.

When you vacate the bathroom, you have
merely had a shower – no-one knows that
you have also cleansed your soul.

At the risk of sounding a bit mad, I find this
helps me to get things out of my system

THE SON

I saw him that evening walking slowly up
the hill, hands in the pockets of his jeans;
just a young lad about eighteen. His hair
was dampened by the drizzle. I passed him
on my way down to the Chinese Takeaway
and only glimpsed him for a moment.

Was he dejected or just weary? Had he had
an argument at home and gone out to
escape, had he got the worries of the world
on his shoulders or was he just a young
guy going to meet a friend?

He could have been *my* son. I wondered in
that moment whether another mother was
passing *my* son in another Country
somewhere across the world and thinking
the same thoughts about him.

This poem was written a couple of months
after my son had gone off travelling abroad

TWIN TOWERS

What terrifying trickery has touched the
world? Its tentacles of destruction trickle
through humanity and traumatize with
terror. With tantalizing treachery, they
teach the tyranny of fanaticism transferring
down the centuries like a ticking time
bomb. Television transmits today and
speculates about tomorrow. The tacit
approval is tempered with criticism,
constantly resurrecting the reasons for the
terrible tragedy - the toppling of the World
Trade Centre, torn down by hypnotic
terrorists. Transatlantic telephones
transmit tortuous messages imploring
restraint, reiterating diplomatic channels,
but this tenuous connection has its
limitations. The resolution has to be
tumultuous. Attractive and evocative seem
the words of war – attack, destroy, defeat.
Forgotten are the tears of abject failure, the
trampled torsos of the dead. Forgotten is
the drought and devastation strewn across
the terrain; the tarpaulin tents of refugees,
so depleted are their lives, taken to the
brink of destruction. The Taliban titillate,
taunting the titanic who, in search of
'truth', take their own retrograde steps
towards tyranny; they too violate by
revenge. Too late will they re-evaluate,
when destitution is revisited? Would
talking have overcome the monster better
than stalking – or will the tyrant of
terrorism still survive?

*Written 29 October 2001 following the attack
on the World Trade Centre on 11 September*

POPPY DAY

Another Remembrance Day Service
And we all hang our heads
The politicians feign sadness
Whilst at the same time
Plotting to send more
Soldiers to die
More mothers to cry
And all for a lie
Which they cannot deny
Or justify
As hard as they try
And out of the silence
The bell tolls
Why....why....why?

*This poem was written in November 2004,
against the background of the Iraq War.*

FOOD

Don't you just get fed up with cooking
And thinking up menus each day?
No sooner is one meal over
Than another is on the way

We're bombarded by news on the media
Saying we must study our diet
But if you keep serving up salads
You're running the risk of a riot

It's so hard to maintain the passion
To get in a cordon bleu mood
When you're in the state
That you want to lose weight
But all you must think of is food

So how do you ring the changes
Whilst balancing cost and time?
Do you shop till you drop in your lunch hour
Or do you just order on line?

Cont ....

Having overcome that major hurdle
Of procuring the ingredients to cook
You have to find time to prepare it
And consulting your recipe book

So now you have finally cooked it
And cleared all the dishes away
But as soon as you put the dishwasher on
Your thoughts have to turn to next day

So how do you solve the dilemma
Of filling our bodies with fuel?
Well, I think I have found the answer
Which has now become my golden rule

When they all come home starving hungry
And into the kitchen they troop
The best thing to give them to fill them all up
Is a nice steaming bowl of hot soup

So when they've all eaten a plenty
And you ask them what they'd like to follow
With a bit of luck, they'll all be full up
And you get a reprieve....... till tomorrow

You can understand why some of us resort to
convenience foods now and again!

POTS

Pretty pomander pots, purple and pink
Sitting proud beneath the window
Porous pots which take in
The ancient atmosphere around
And pour out the centuries
Like pictures passing through your mind
Pure and simple in form
And blessed by the passage of time

*I was once asked to write a poem on the
subject of Pots and this is what came out*

SUGAR

Oh *why* do they have to spill sugar
All over the kitchen worktop?
Would it be so hard
To just laden the spoon
And tip it straight into the cup?

No – spread it around seems the motto
When sweetening their coffee or tea
Or when covering a mountain of cereal
A snowcap of sugar runs free

Just shed a bit here
And shed a bit there
I know that they
Just do not think

But when *I've* cleaned up for the
thousandth time
And shot it straight into the sink
I do so despair to get anywhere
By asking them *nicely* to think

It's such a small thing to worry about
I suppose that I shouldn't get cross
But if it's so easy to clear up the mess
So why then can't *they* wield the cloth!

I wrote this poem as a bit of
fun really, trying to get my message
across in a humorous way!

THE HAND

Dear hand
Why do you ail so?
Are you fatigued
By years of lifting and turning?
You once were elegant
Adorned by red polish and rings
Cosseted by creams
And admired by many
Flirtatious in your movement
Expressive to extremes
Caressing and adoring
Faces that have been
Years of heavy shopping
Years of cooking fare
Years of changing nappies
And of brushing hair
Years of cleaning toilets
And dusting everywhere
Years of pushing cleaners
And carrying up the stairs
But now you are so painful
No-one can really care
When all you've done for others
Just leaves you hanging there

It is perhaps not until we experience
this sort of pain that we appreciate
how debilitating it is

RESCUE YOUR BODY

I'm rescuing my body
Before it is too late
I really have just let things go
To get into this state
I'm on a downward spiral
At such a rapid rate
So I'm rescuing my body
Before it is too late
So now I'm forced to exercise
To halt my ageing gait
And join with others in the class
To whom I can relate
So here we sit upon the floor
All prisoners of our fate
Trying to find the wherewithal
So we can activate
Muscles we forgot we had
Which help us to abate
Osteoporosis or similar complaint
We're determined to confront it
And not capitulate
So we're rescuing our bodies
Before it is too late

*I wrote this poem about our 50+ exercise
class which goes under this title*

IN THIS GARDEN

In this garden I feel safe
Amongst the majestic trees
So solid and dependable
The leaves speak to me
And flowers smile upon me

I came here for comfort
For no particular reason
Just because I felt I needed
Something to enfold me

The plants mingle in drifts of colour
To captivate the eye
And the butterflies dance among them
The kind sun warms me
And makes me feel loved again

I close my eyes
And hear the crows gathering overhead
But even this does not disturb my tranquillity
I have found the peace I was seeking
And feel loved in this garden

*I wrote this poem on a beautiful August day
in the garden of an old vicarage, after seeing
my young son off to France*

THE SPIDER'S WEB

I am the spider
You are my prey
I'm quietly watching you
Coming my way
Into my web
So beautifully spun
To lure you in
And give me my fun
With intricate patterns
I'm casting my spell
Enticing you inwards
And out of your shell
I'm expert you see
At setting a trap
I know you'll succumb
Because you're a chap
Inside my web
You'll soon be entwined
And then I will have you
Body and mind

*On considering how some
women can manipulate men*

SEIZE THE MOMENT

I'm a mother and a wife
Been a daughter all my life
But I've reached the age, you see
When I'm trying to think of me
I'd better make it quick
I mustn't miss a trick
I have to find the room
To catch myself in bloom
Or I will miss the moment
If I should stop to dither
And all my fragile petals
Will start to wilt and wither
It's vital that I find myself
And do not hesitate
Or more responsibilities
Will deem it far too late

*After you have brought up the children
you suddenly realise that you should
sandwich in some time for yourself before
you have to take on other responsibilities*

WERE WE TO PART

I wonder, were we to part, would I be the
sort of woman with whom it would rankle,
who would wither away and wilt on the vine
wishing that things could have been
different, boring her friends and shrinking
her soul with bitterness and reproach?

Or would I be a glorious voluptuous woman
full of courage and bravery, inventive in
reprisal and revelling in the rewards of
sweet revenge?

I wonder, what would I be?

*This piece was inspired by Lady Sarah
Graham-Moon who cut the arms from her
husband's Savile Row suits, ransacked his
wine cellar and threw paint on his BMW car
when she believed him to have been
unfaithful*

CUPBOARD LOVE

The utility cupboard tells the story
Of days gone by and all the glory
Of penalty shoot outs cheered by dads
Of rugby tackles and other fads
The football boot dubbin
And white sports gel
They each of them have
Their own tale to tell
Of cold winter mornings
In pouring rain
We only just made it
Too late up again
The remonstration
Of parent to child
The shouting and screaming
That drove you both wild
The sense of excitement
When scoring that goal
The hugging and kissing
Or time to console
All of those memories
So bound up with care
The utility cupboard
Still holds them in there

*It is amazing how supportive parents can
be to their children's sporting activities!*

CLOTHES

Why is it that you have to spread
Your clothes all over the floor?
It's got to the point
That try as I might
I can hardly
Get inside your door

I don't want to moan
Whenever you're home
I'd prefer to make time more productive
But it seems the temptation
To litter your floor
Has become for you rather seductive

So now and again I'll bury my pride
And tidy it into neat piles
But then I am caught
By an ironic thought
That I *miss* the mess of my child!

*It is perhaps a quirk of human nature
that often the things which aggravated
us are those which we miss*

STRICTLY COME DANCING

I'll go on Strictly Come Dancing
And knock 'em out with me frocks
Like a bird I will soar
Around the dance floor
In a Waltz or dainty Foxtrot

My Cha Cha Cha
Will be quite stunning
With intricate foot work quite cunning
They'll hip hip hooray
At my Paso Doble
And I know I'll be up in the running

My Samba will be oh so sexy
The Rumba will drive them all wild
And after my Tango
I'll dance the Fandango
And have 'em all out in the aisles

Yes I dream I'm on Strictly Come Dancing
And I'm up there with Brucie and Tess
Having danced through the night
I wake up with a fright -
The bed's in a *hell* of a mess!

Like lots of other people, I really enjoyed the
Series which made me wish I could dance

COVER UP CHRISTMAS

Why not cover up for Christmas
And pretend that we're ok?
We can bury all the baggage
It's only for one day
We can stuff it in the turkey
And boil it with the sprouts
We can simmer with the mulled wine
And never let it out
We can chitter chitter chatter
And open with delight
If only we can keep it up
Until the close of night
And after goodbye kisses
And the shutting of the door
We'll then continue with our lives
The way they were before

*It is often said that Christmas can be
a very difficult time for relationships!*

AT THE GYM

We went to the Gym, you see
My arms, my legs and me
We've got to the stage
Of that difficult age
When our tummy just wants to hang free

So to the Gym we thought we'd go
And start things off gently and slow
We cycled sedately
Our posture was stately –
We kept our dignity though

The next was the walking machine
(Or running, if you're very keen)
We surveyed the surroundings
Of young people's poundings
(To avoid the reflection of me)

Then we moved on to the rowing
Our rhythm now pleasantly flowing
We sat at our ease
Watching our knees
Up and down, coming and going

Cont'd ....

Next came a frightening machine
For tummy tightening, it seemed
Like an electric chair
We sat down in there
To execute till we were lean

The next to address was the waist
Turning our body and face
Twisting the chair
Until we got there
Then controlling it back into place

And finally, the lower back
We sat up to take up the slack
Like a shampooist's chair
When they're washing your hair
And you think that your neck's going to crack

So now we have had our induction
On machines that should help our reduction
To a much smaller size
Round the tummy and thighs
But if *that* fails, we'll try Liposuction!

On a whim, I went to the gym for an
induction and then, of course, wrote a silly
poem about the experience

THE BUZZARD

You draw me like a magnet to the spot
where you hide, amongst the wooded cover
across the field, and my eyes keenly scan
the branches searching for your elusive
form.

But even as I catch a glimpse, you have
flown, skimming the brown earth, which
lends to your disguise. So shy you are in
your magnificence, defying my prying eyes.

Then all at once you are above me. High in
the sky you fly, soaring on the thermals,
displaying your lighter side. With powerful
pride you glide round and round, from side
to side.

An effortless thrust gives speed to your
flight and, hard as I try, I can no longer spy
your elegant form in the sunkissed sky.
You have gone from my eye, but still your
beauty lies held within my mind.

*There are certain days, when the weather
conditions are right, that you just know you
will see a buzzard and when you do, it is
magical.*

TEXTING

Texting is great
When you are running late
Or to tell someone you care
When you just cannot be there

You can send love and affection
Or give someone directions
Wish good luck in exams
When your mobile's in your hands

Texting gives you freedom
When you are full of worry
To avoid a conversation
Or if you're in a hurry

It's a way of saying sorry
And I love you very much
But most of all it's brilliant
For just keeping in touch

*Just after writing this poem, I heard
on the News that there is now a
recognised addiction to mobile phones,
for which people are receiving therapy!*

ON THEIR LEAVING HOME

And so I enter another new phase of my
life. A phase without children at home. So
strange it is, so quiet. Music no longer
wafts along corridors, doors no longer bang,
showers no longer wurr. No mess, no
shouting, no laughter, no fun. Life glides
along seamlessly with only the occasional
ripple of humour or argument.

When it happens, you cannot believe it is
that time. You cannot recognise it. There
is this sudden dawning that they have
gone, without your really knowing it. Sure,
they've been away before – stayed with
friends, had holidays, gone travelling, but
always you know they will be back.

But this time it is different. They've made
commitments elsewhere, created a new life
for themselves away from you. It is that
realisation that is hard to come to terms
with when for years you have been their
base, you have been the ones they have
come home to, you have been the ones to
hear their stories of where they have been
and whom they have met and you have still
felt like an anchor in their lives.

Cont'd ....

People try to console you by saying you must have done a good job in order for them to feel confident enough to go, and you agree but, initially, in your heart you feel a sense of loss. A career helps, offering a distraction from thought, but nothing ever fills the void of their presence, their music or their messiness that you moaned about when they were at home. Ironically, it is often those very things that you miss, and therein lies the guilt. Could you have been different? Could you have been more understanding? Yes, you probably could, but you just did your best at the time, given all the circumstances, which perhaps were not always easy. And, on reflection, that is what life is all about, that is why they are now equipped to leave, because they *have* experienced it all with you – the ups and downs, the fun and the despair, the laughter and the arguments.

So don't feel bad about it all. Just look upon it as another inevitable phase of parenting to which you will soon adjust

THE OMELETTE MAN

The Omelette Man slammed the pan
Cursing as the telephone rang
He got himself in such a state
As omelettes slid from pan to plate
Utensils flew into the air
The knives and forks went everywhere
My temper then began to flare
As I became irate

When all that he had had to do
Was simply say "There's a call for you"
Instead he did initiate
A moody meal, then served up late
In stony silence then we ate
And so his temper sealed his fate
For my advice, which should be heeded
Was that more practise was what he needed!

*My husband offered to cook that particular
evening whilst I washed my car, and this
was the outcome! Later in the evening,
I just couldn't resist writing this poem.*

MUM

My mother, I love her
But I sometimes forget
That I really should treat her
With a bit more respect
For she's been a daughter
A mother and wife
With responsibilities
All of her life
She's so independent
And still very glam
So I really appreciate
How lucky I am
To have such a mum
Who's always been there
And I want her to know
That I do really care

*Maybe sometimes I have taken
my Mum for granted, so this one's
for her, to say thanks*

LIKE WE USED TO

Let's go out tonight
Like we used to
Let's talk and look into each other's eyes
Like we used to
Let's pretend we know nothing of each other
But we want to know more
To discover all those little things
That we *now* know
If we had known them all then
Would we have changed our minds?
No, it's still good
And we are still on a road of discovery with
each other

In a long-term relationship, it's easy to
become complacent so perhaps we should
make more time for each other

THE FACE

It gets harder every day
To keep those big bad bags away
Concealer now no longer works
To hide dark rings which seem to lurk
Beneath those eyes which once shone bright
But now look forward to the night
When softer hues then find a way
To flatter more than in the day

This comes to us all as we get older
but I believe that we must make the
best of ourselves

MENOPAUSE

Be at peace with yourself. Remember, your body is undoing the wonderful process of reproduction in its own complicated and unpredictable way.

Hard as it is, you must put your trust in nature. In the same miraculous way that your body created your children, you now have to allow it to perform the final miracle of menopause.

You can endeavour to ease the passage with potions but you cannot deny it this ultimate crescendo.

I wrote this to remind myself that the menopause is a natural process and to be more relaxed about it

GETTING OLD

When I am gnarled and old and grey
Please don't look down on me and say
"She doesn't know the time of day"
For once, I organized your life
I was a mother and a wife

*When I wrote this, I had in mind all
those elderly ladies in retirement
homes who sometimes get treated
with disdain*

Wherever possible, surround yourself with fun. Laugh, from the bottom of your heart, *real* laughter that sterilises your body and relaxes your soul. Only certain people can do this for you, and if you find them, treasure them as friends as they are *very* valuable. Good looks seem important but you can understand why a beautiful sunny personality is often just as appealing. It is an enduring gift, above all riches, which is delightfully infectious to others when given the right conditions of incubation.

I wrote this on considering how great it is to have a good laugh with friends and this is my tribute to them